Bo
and the Kite

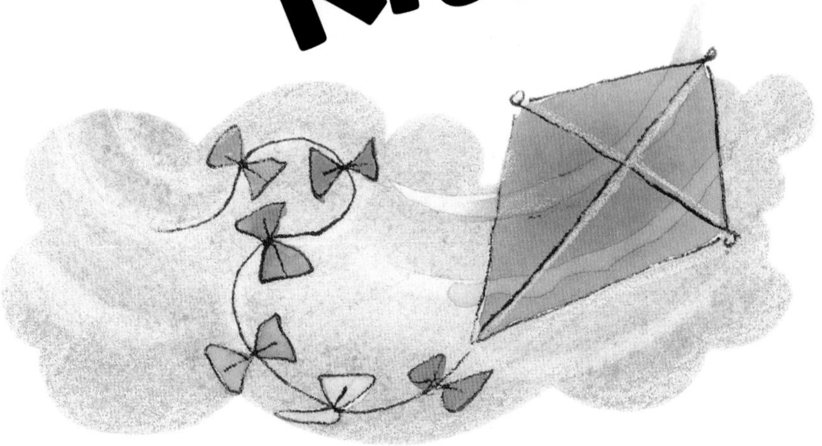

Monica Hughes
Illustrated by Lisa Smith

Rigby
A Harcourt Achieve Imprint

www.Rigby.com
1-800-531-5015

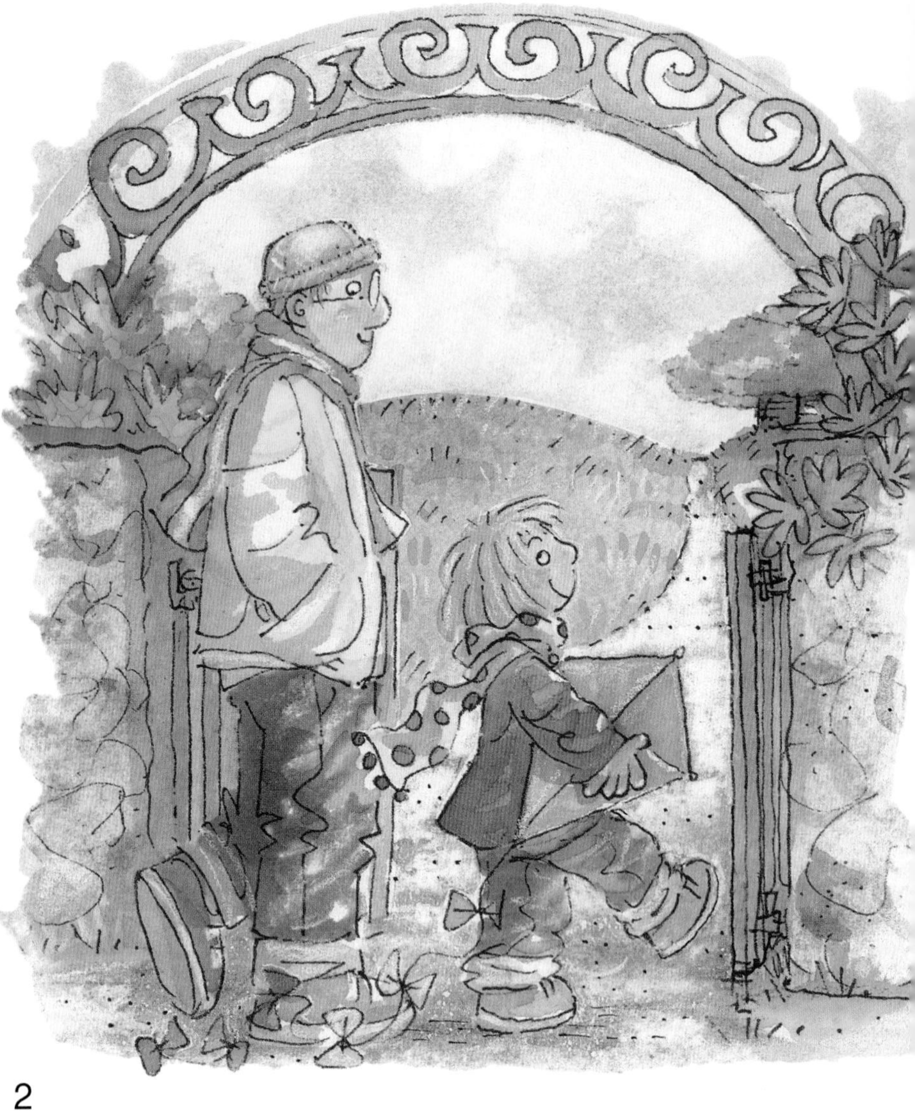

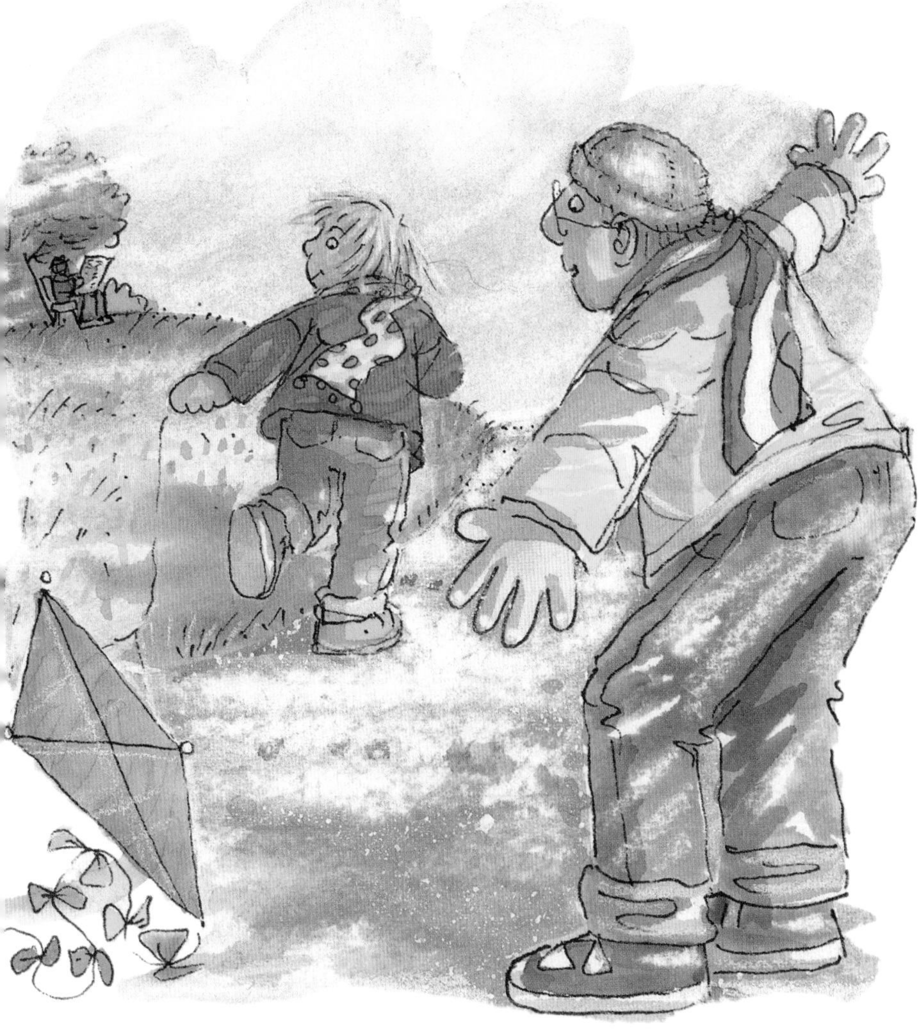

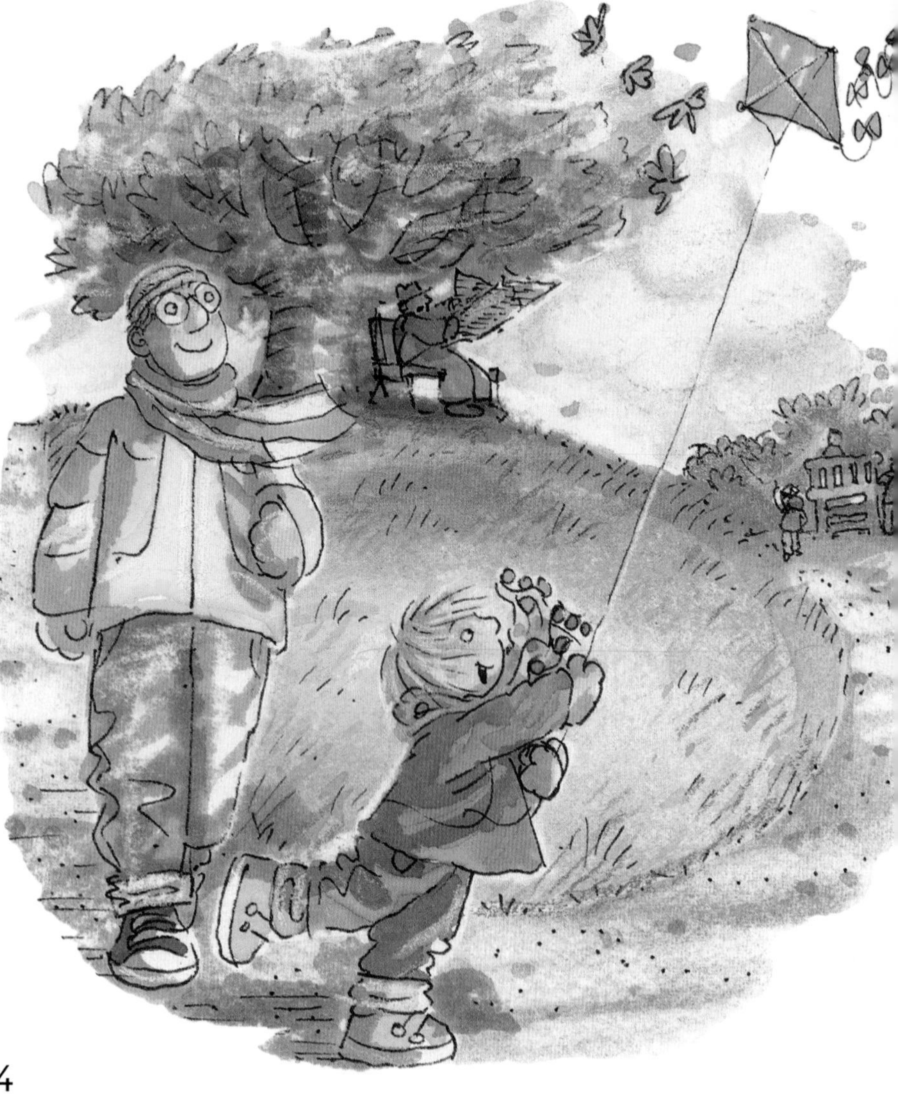

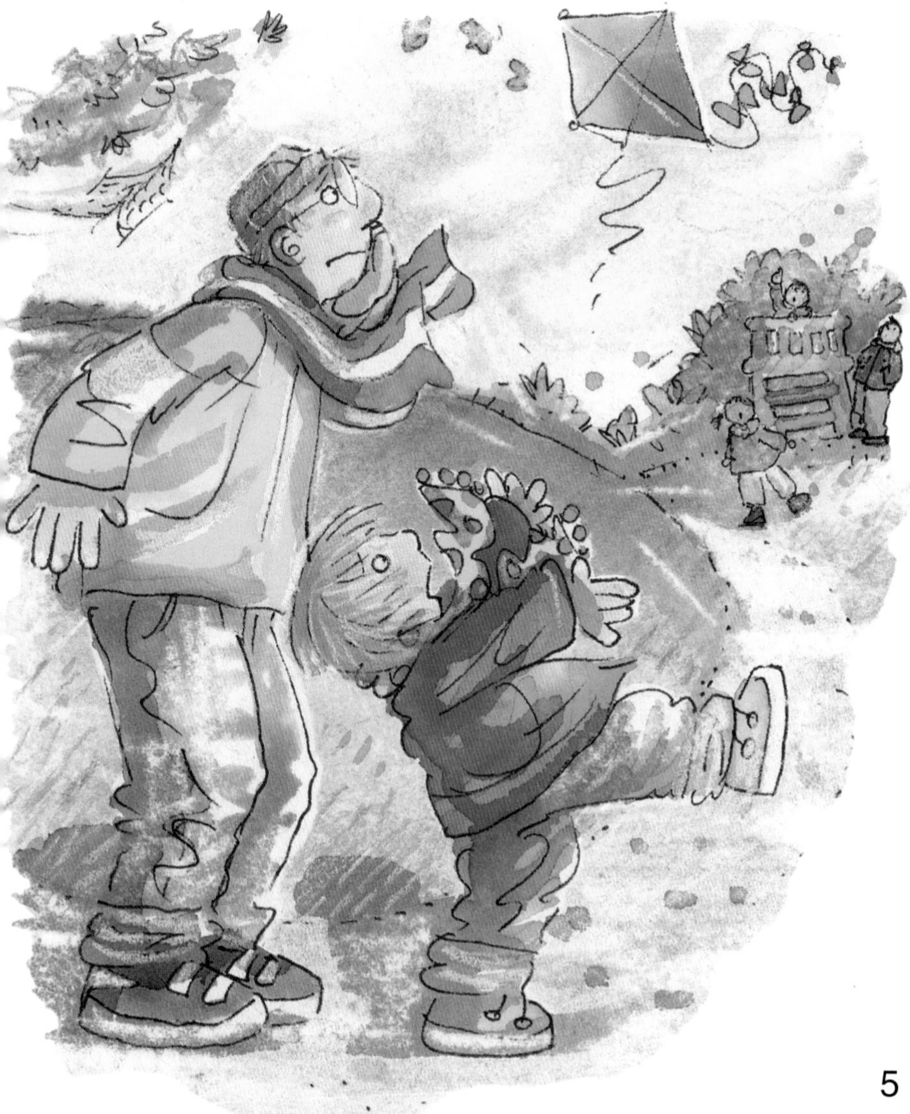

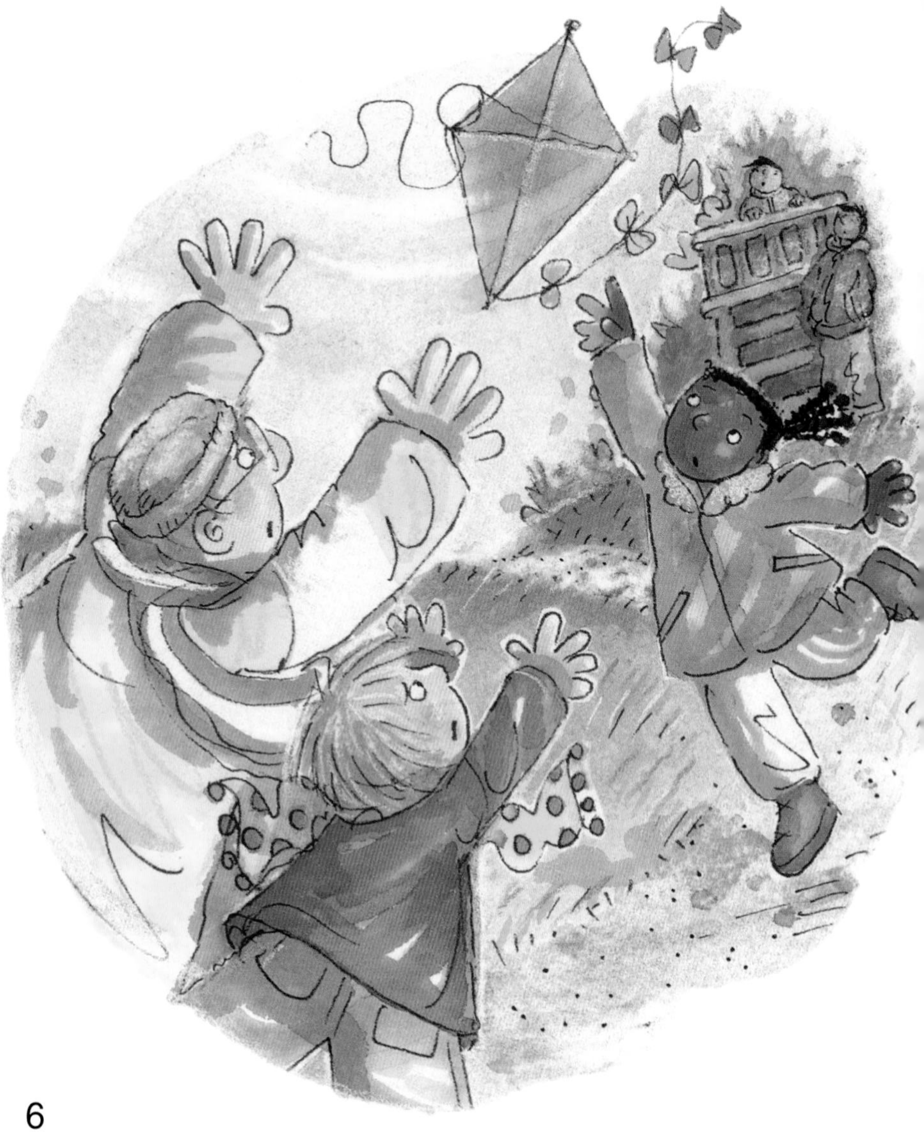

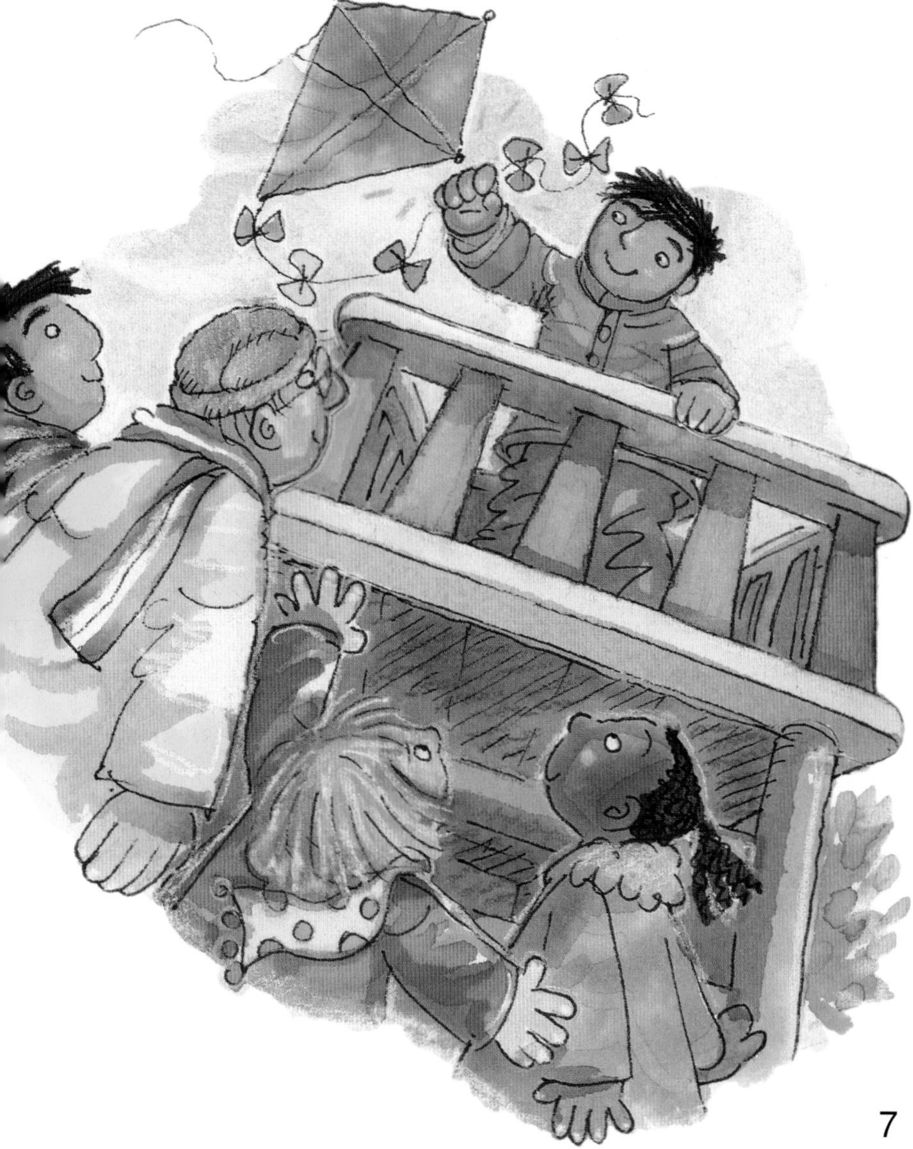

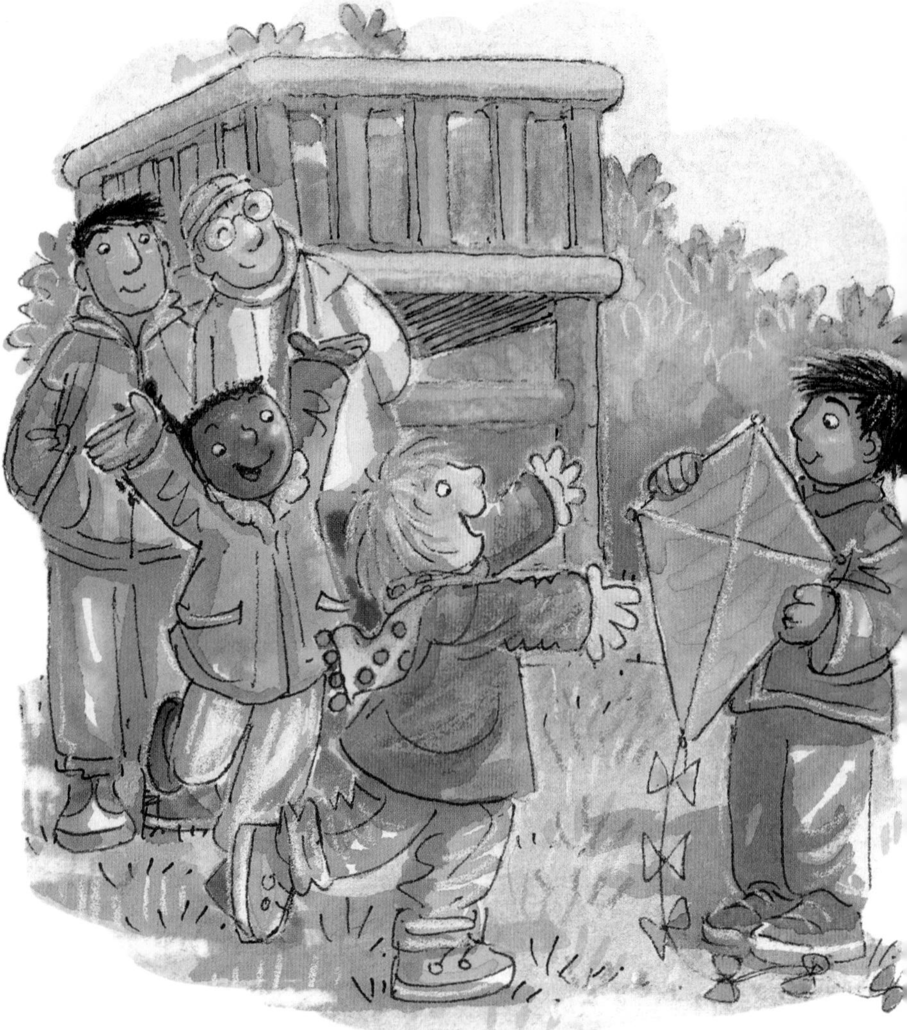